Quiet Musings

Quiet Musings

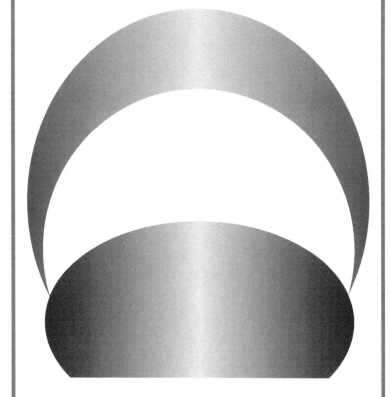

Rolland G. Smith

Sun-Scape Publications

Stamford · Toronto

Canadian Cataloguing in Publication Data

Smith, Rolland G., 1941-
    Quiet musings

Poems.
ISBN 0-919842-22-4

I. Title.

PS3569.M5378Q54 1995   811' .54   C95-931981-6

Sun-Scape Publications
A Division of Sun-Scape Enterprises Limited
65 High Ridge Road, Suite 103
Stamford, Connecticut 06905, USA

P.O. Box 793, Station "F"
Toronto, Ontario M4Y 2N7, Canada

Design by Megan MacQueen, Graphic-Painting-Grids
Photographs by Sheila Ryan

Printed in the United States of America

Dedication

To the Tinkerbell of the One verse
that knows the hidden
and sees it as a gift.

California 1995

Contents

Foreword

It is said that man should reside in reason and move in passion. In this collection of poems by Rolland G. Smith, one finds such a balance. With his creativity and honesty, which serve to link the spiritual and the sensual, we are transported to places and feelings which are at once strangely familiar, a universal remembrance of time, place, and emotion. A winter, a spring; a garden, a seashore; a love, an anguish, a joy.

These are the elements of the poetry you will find here, along with poems which speak of the complexity of our relationships with our Earth's creatures, our children and ourselves.

Through his words, we are allowed a glimpse into the spirit of a man whose career has taken him to many people and places around the world, and has contributed to a poetry which takes us all to a place Yeats called "the deep heart's core."

~ Sheila Ryan
San Diego, California
1995

Preface

One might rightfully ask what inspires a broadcast journalist to dwell in Aeonian words. The quick answer is balance. The long answer involves acknowledging the heart, spirit, awareness, and nature.

Each broadcast day contains many of the sorrowful and tragic stories in life. Emphasis is placed on information that separates our unique human nature into undesirable parts. We have labeled them as hate, prejudice, violence, intolerance, and greed, yet all of them are the children of fear.

These characteristics exist within each of us, but it is through the benevolent experience called life that we are presented with unlimited opportunities to eliminate fear from our active consciousness and to see ourselves, our communities, our nations, and eventually our world as shared joy.

Poetry returns separation to wholeness. It de-emphasizes the "di-" of diversity and amplifies the "verse" of inclusion. Verse is the poetry of life, the rhyme of reason, the sonnet of similarities, and it should be the meter of the media.

This is the practical choice for me, and in that choice comes the profound awareness that I create my personal environment by what I think, and I cocreate my professional environment by the stories I tell. I use poetry and prose under the aegis of commentary to offer an alternative view of man and nature.

Poetry encourages the reader and the writer to tune into the inner side of life and story and to see the illusion as well as the Reality of Being. I invite you to join me there.

~ Rolland G. Smith

A special tribute and grateful appreciation to
Mr. Kenneth G. Mills, a teacher, a friend, a
Mahatma who precipitates creative grace from
the Source and gives it unconditionally
to anyone who asks. I did!
Thank you!

Acknowledgements

Thank you to Ellen Mann, Megan MacQueen,
and Sheila Ryan for their selfless efforts, special talent,
and artistic encouragement.

poems

Sacred Space

In morning walk, around a bend,
    a sacred place I found
With ancient trees to guard it
    their strength secure to ground.

Nurtured by a mother Earth,
    Oaken arms create the nest,
A space of peace, a leafy place
    where itinerant spirits rest.

Braiding branches of wooden warmth
    entwine an interlacing loom,
Weaving nature's natural grace
    into a passage to a room.

A chambered vale of living oak,
    soothing eye and troubled mind.
There is a welcome comfort here,
    and I walk this bending wynd.

A carpet tan of earthen hues
    and scattered fallen leaves,
Sunlight ripples on the dell,
    patterns wrinkled by the breeze.

I know this place comes from above,
    reflecting light that's pure.
A harmony, a resonance,
    a healing to endure.

October Mild

O October, thou transit month of eight,
    did I lose you? Was I late?
I searched a branch and on the ground,
    no crunchy leaves in colors found.

If it's gone, this season all,
    I can recall a festooned fall
Of crimson trees and ochre leaves
    floating in a sienna breeze.

I would not miss it! If it were me!
    A time in life of mystery.
Feeling like a youthful green,
    yet with memories to redeem.

How do you tell those of Spring,
    hope eternal will always bring
A bud of life and growing flowers
    to beautify the tolling hours.

There is joy in Spring and Fall
    and Summer's treat and Winter's call.
Life is seasons, designed to be
    creation for eternity.

Erosion

Water carves an open slice
    in earthen crust to view
Roots of Trees, in sacrifice,
    dangling, drying, all askew.

Stand beside this suckled swath,
    see nursing roots entwined,
Weaving deep in mineral path
    probing rock with stone enshrined.

A single root does no good
    holding life secure to ground
Lacing tight is understood
    to free the green unbound.

Behold the bold of other roots
    and the strength they give as one,
Many mingled braided shoots
    stay earth from water's run.

There is a truth in nature's cut,
    how helping gives a strength,
Protecting from eroding rut
    so life can have its length.

Erosion speaks not a word,
    yet its language is precise.
The wisdom of the undergird,
    for man, is sound advice.

Doorknob

How useful is this holding point that
decorates a door with brass.
It helps us to enter and to leave
      sometimes alone and oft en masse.

When smooth and round in simple chrome,
      It turns and locks and latches tight
But rarely gets its honor due
      when carved of wood or crystal bright.

Next time you open a closed door
      reflect upon protruding knob
In varied shapes and styles vast;
      give thanks for this thingamabob.

Raven's Call

I found a way to see forever
　　through the window of the sea.
Liquid light — reflecting sun,
　　changing, changing, ever free.

Then a Raven called my name
　　as he flew in currents fair.
Soaring over canyon routes
　　he said, "Do you dare?!"

I tried to understand his thought,
　　remembering the past,
Then out from me my spirit sprang
　　free from body cast.

The breath of flight took my heart,
　　then sent it back to me
In waves of gentle surfing sound
　　as I glided to the sea.

The Raven sailed to my side
　　and we flew beyond together,
Never fearing up or down,
　　our spirits linked forever.

What lessons here for me to learn
　　from Raven black and sleek:
Trust will be the freedom
　　to finally take the leap!

Sea Truth

Shimmering Sea — azure shades of sky,
    ripples in a mirror, reflection of a high.
There's distant blue and nearer green
    experienced first — then clearly seen.

Close your eyes and feel the breeze,
    an ocean gift, her nature pleased.
This landward wind from blue beyond
    brings saline songs of tidal pond.

With bursting puffs of curling surf
    the salted manna seeks the turf.
In respect the two abide
    as they struggle side by side.

Yet rolling waves reclaim the sand
    that once was called a part of land,
Then washing rain erodes the earth
    to claim a patch of greater worth.

Could it be true for people too,
    to share another point of view?
The ocean brings us many truths —
    find its meaning, see its proof.

Dolphin Cage

I saw them swim with slippery grace
    bounding, bobbing in gentle chase.
In pairs they moved without complaint,
    aware, the pool with cage constraint.
Clucking talk and slapping splash
    playful, loving, in their dash.
But might they wish, from heart within,
    seaward freedom for all Dolphin.

Mankind pretends a noble mind,
    yet holds encaged another kind,
In zoos and tanks — incarcerate,
    alleged to train and educate.
We think we are the higher one
    but we're the species others shun.
What will it take to change our mind
    and let us see where we've been blind?

Cloaks of fur or scale or skin
    it matters not, for we are kin,
Creations of a primal God,
    part of sea and part of sod.
Each day the count of species lost
    is measured in a human cost,
For gifts are gone that are a cure
    of illness strange by serum pure.

Dolphins tell us with their eyes
    what soul within should realize,
That intellect and reasoning
    may only bring a reckoning.
We must embrace the cosmic mind
    and not enslave another kind.
We must embrace the cosmic heart
    to loose the ties that keep us part.

Black Beauty

Take first the black from ebon night
　　and add the dark of eyeless sight.
Create a canvas of your mind,
　　then paint upon this lightless find.
Some only see the dun of dark,
　　others know what black can spark,
For in the ink of soot abyss
　　is all the brighten sheen of bliss.
Extract the color from this face
　　to see the beauty in that place.
Kind thoughts of red and service blue
　　bring from the black its color true.
Add loving hues in layered stroke
　　and watch the darkness shed its cloak.
If thoughts are colors made of light
　　and flare from spirit's aura bright,
Then think the rainbow that you are
　　and know your soul as avatar.

Instinct

A blossom blooms from 'neath the sticks
ascending to a raying sun,
Reaching, teaching all the rest,
    that trying lets it be the one.

It cares not how it started there
    nor if the frost will take its bite.
Its instinct finds the noble path
    to move between and find the light.

It shares the water and the ground,
    no drop nor space more than it needs.
Between the rocks on stony crust
    first it flowers, and then it seeds.

The splendor of the leafy plant
    belies the dry and sandy loam.
The beauty found within the seed
    will find a place to make a home.

How can it be that we don't see
    this could be true for humankind?
The gift within each living soul
    seeks shaped expression nonaligned.

City Walk

I walked around the city block,
    a winter shiver shook unkind.
A homeless man lay 'neath a grate
    to warm his body, then his mind.
His hopeless bend wrapped 'round himself,
    reminding me of passions felt,
That wind around awakened heart
    when bodies' chill begins to melt.
It may be choice or circumstance,
    but I am lonely and feeling sad,
My sad is mood and his is need,
    yet both are cold with hope unclad.
Lonely comes from self-creation,
    for matter formed will follow thought.
Could I change it? Were it so,
    my mind would cringe at what it wrought.
Whose pain is worse and bottomless:
    the one who wants or one in need?
I cannot tell by walking by.
    I cannot tell who will succeed.

Changing Light

I remember as a child
   when the light out in the hall
Came creeping through an oaken door
   and made the shadows tall.

The bureau was a monster,
   the mirror a gaping hole.
My toys began to scare me,
   as the covers held my soul.

In older years and wiser ones
   there shines another light.
This time it comes from spirit
   and does not carry fright.

My mind now has the freedom
   to see a brightness clear.
To know that I am always safe
   I must let go of fear.

Canyon Walk

My walk began at canyon's rim, beneath an
autumn sky.
The morning air was crisp, and dust came from
the dry.
I looked around at nature, knowing I would find
Her rhythm in a rock, and reason in her rhyme.

I heard it first on the path, walking, slowly not
too far.
It faded in and out of mind, like a distant
twinkling star.
Then louder came its gentle tone, uniquely
humming mild,
When tuning clear to nature's sound, your spirit
is beguiled.

You know it in the sparkle of a trickling tiara
stream
That slides o'er stone and granite bead, crowning
Gaia queen.
You feel it in the wilting wind with all its names
that please:
"Refreshing," "Cooling," "Gentle," special kinds
of breeze.

You see it in the flora and the rainbow of the
flower,
As blossoms burst with color in a natural
sculptured bower.
You taste it in her breath when fragrance fills the air,
With tiny pollens of her heart, perfumes of
scented prayer.

Nature's essence is profound, her truth comes when
    you listen
To the dew that's on the grass and hear the sunlight
    glisten.
Squinting crystals in the bright who hide when it is
    warm,
Returning precious liquid life in shower and in storm.

I found it tiny, on the ground, in trails of hurried
    ants.
I found it, too, among the herbs and healing medicine
    plants.
I find it often in the trees, amid a darting of delight
As playful fluttering feathered ones put magic in their
    flight.

There are other things to know, from the silence of
    her breach,
To heed the wise and warning shrill of the owl's
    casting screech.
Nature's sounds speak many tongues to tell us there
    is trouble,
For in the print of humankind, the future reeks in
    rubble.

But on this day, I shall not dwell on the ablutionary
    bad,
For it would change my canyon walk and make my
    smile sad.
In all my walks, on many paths, even ones without a
    tree,
I choose to find the joy of life, for nature lives in me.

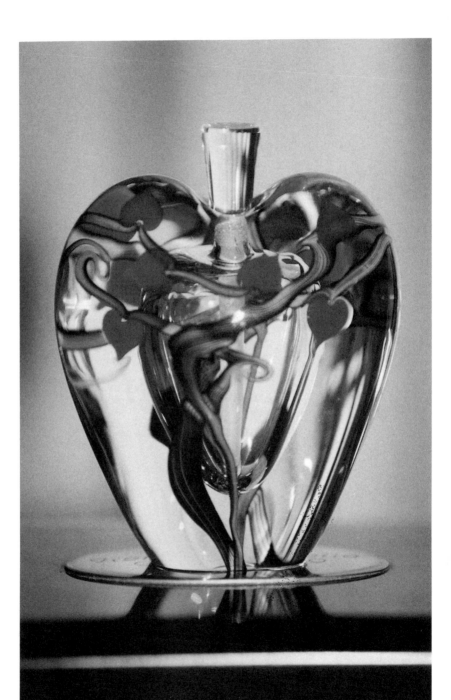

The Gift

It was a dream, I know it was:
    a gossamer gift unwrapping,
revealing pure a pristine path
      of Celtic quare,
      innocence fair.

If not a dream, it could have been.
    Beauty standing au naturel,
giving freely her gift unclothed,
      as heart transcends,
      the mind pretends.

It is a dream, a supple gift
    curving softly, statuesque,
warm in smoothing, soothing white,
      first gowned in green,
      or so it seemed.

But dreams are dreams, and I awake
    to take my leave and not partake
of Beauty's gift, for body ache
      will linger on, but not forsake
      the longing for the dream's remake.

Ocean Moonshine

Melting light from 'neath the waves,
confetti chaff of Lunar shine,
Wrapped in the swell of night's dark tide
are brilliant beams that surf the brine.

Sterling links of silver gleaming,
opalescent and neon glows,
Flickering gleam before wave break
as sparkles churn and glitter flows.

A privileged sight along the shore,
transcending light of ocean sheen
That comes to those who choose to see
when moon is full upon terrene.

Carrizo Wash

A desert vast to see and feel
what is true and what is real.
Streaks and scratches on the land,
no natural lode of thin fahlband.
Its tracks of man — tire scarred,
old bed of sea now wheel marred.
Barren dry, yet full of life,
under rocks of weather's knife
Granite grays and sandy stone
Black basalt and sun-bleached bone
Sages grow in pale hue
when green and cream rendezvous.
Fossil dunes from tranquil past
beneath a sea that didn't last.
Old solitude with crusts of shell,
what ancient day felt your knell?
Thou sacred sweep, what is worse:
no ocean cover or man's traverse?
Intruding sounds in paradise
make this silent place die twice.

Cattails

I listened to a weaving tale,
 whispered soft by waving reeds
Who shyly crown their blossom tops
 with spikes of downy seeds.

Fragrant scents, antennae tuned,
 they cast a beacon call
Beckoning to bird on wind,
 come land on cattail tall.

From thinning air, a blackbird comes
 with red upon her wing,
She lights upon the velvet wick
 and then begins to sing.

"These rushes are the cloth," she says,
 to wash the water clean.
These Oracles of wetland marsh
 return the liquid sheen.

The leaves absorb the summer sun,
 then bask in winter tan
And soon the shuffle of a breeze
 unravels seeds of panne.

The tiny fertile sailing seeds
 soon tack on upward drafts,
Drifting to the moistened ground
 near slivered sentient shafts.

In time the kitten seedlings rise,
 in clustered sentry stand,
And grow to be the story
 in this tale of watered land.

Christmas Time

Christmas time surprises as it
    jumps out from the cold
To warm the late December days with
    frankincense and gold,
It heralds in with music in the silent of
    the night,
And when it wakes the child within,
    my memories are all bright.

Happy thoughts are set to play this darkest
    time of light
And brighten up the shortened days with
    friends who reunite.
Chums of old and pals of new, all wishing
    Christmas cheer,
With cedar sparks from glowing logs to
    warm the midnight clear.

It's wrapping hearts in holly green and
    Rudolph red with bow
And standing 'neath a berried sprig of
    kissing mistletoe.
Dancing dreams of sugarplums and
    minted candy cane
Bring visions of a Christmas tree and a
    circling tooting train.

There's spruce to cut and wreaths to make
    in circles and in sprays
that decorate the doors and hearths on
    merry Noel days.

There's lights to string, and wood to
    bring, and ornaments to make
For packages beneath the tree, as snow
    begins to flake.

I harken as the angels sing, with distant
    family near,
And I love to hear a child say the names
    of eight reindeer.
Patina thoughts of Christmas past and
    shiny ones of new
Remind me of the Magi three and a child
    named *Jesu.*

There's jingle bells and icicles and
    packages to tie
With ribbons tight and wrappings bright,
    of sleighs up in the sky.
There's hugs galore and candy more and
    kids with favorite toys
And shirts and socks and building blocks
    for little girls and boys.

There's cards and calls and carols,
    and candles fill the room,
And tins of sugar cookies shine by red
    poinsettia bloom.
Christmas time indeed surprises in a
    special wondrous way;
In winter and forever, it's my favorite
    holiday.

Freedom

Forever to be free
    the choice is to be.
The I that you see
    is not what is me.

The Me that is free
    is a part of thee.
When I choose to be,
    the I sees as we.

The Call

I called, it rang, and you're not there!
    Why does it seem that it's not fair
That you are gone, when I need you
    to talk of love and moments true?

It is a feeling, some call love,
    exemplified by cooing dove
Appearing soft in mind with hope,
    blending as the two elope.

It's hard for me when you're not there
    relaxing in your rocking chair —
A place I love, but cannot claim,
    before the hearth and warming flame.

I know I am not near to you,
    but I am close enough to view
The panorama of the heart
    that aches a tear when we're apart.

El Corazón

Por ella yo doy mi corazón,
    and the inner spirit of my life.
Her gift of loving friendship alone
    is ecstasy graced with lovers rife.

Be forever mindful of the now,
    its sanguine truth uncased from the start,
Leaping from its rhythmic source to vow:
    "Te amo, Te amo, my sweetheart."

Empty Hand

The hearth is cold, no fire warms
    to stay the chill of inner storms.
Spent wood is carved and charred by flame
    that gave a warmth to stranger's claim.
It must have been a fire bright
    as one hand held the other's tight,
For I can feel the love that stays
    when 'twas said, "Let me count the ways."
Mind ashes leap from memory
    when you cannot be near to me.
Their waning glow, tho bright in thought,
    reminds me of what absence wrought:
An ache within heart's fire bold,
    for I don't have your hand to hold.

Desert Rain

I heard, a sound
    that's been away,
Tho part of someone else's day.

Splattering the ground
    in cadenced time,
Each drop — harmony — in rhyme.

My body, feeling rain
    a pleasured sigh,
Remembering when it was not dry.

A moment only — gone again,
    A memory, in the damp.
Wet! Until the sun's dry lamp.

Garden Grace

Two blossoms yellow, proud above the green,
   stand strong and know their love is seen
By all who wander and by those who gaze
     into this garden of wonder, a maze.
Color binds attention and form holds grace
     attracting heart and spirit to this place.
The flowers stand as one and separate too,
     symbols of the noble ones, too few.
They come to see and hold this place in love,
     responding to an essence from above.
The nectar is the wine the flowers hold,
     toasting through the touch of zephyr's gold.
Tell all strangers who pass here, walking by:
     The fragrance of the flowers glorifies
The spirit of the earth and nurtured seed
     that blossoms into beauty when we need.

Fireplace Chairs

Two empty leather chairs
    hold warm a fire's heat.
The flame is firm and glowing,
    crackling burn — smoke bestowing
Blessings upon the burgundy, buttoned
    spirits of the hearth.
Blameless tongues of blaze.
    Its light empowers
    as flame devours.
It's sad the chairs are empty.

Exhibit

She stood there in the room
    an artist — She.
    Wondering!
Paintings from her tomb of light,
    bright, slight colors soft,
    auras of the darkness of her womb.
Each canvas — a price of more than marked.
Cost is measured in consumption.
Yet creation comes again
    for art is self-redemption.

Wind

Invisible by day and night
 tho Presence felt of gentle might
Until the time of raging storm
 and rain becomes a pelting swarm.

It is the wind I tell about,
 caressing soft or howling shout.
It can't be seen when all alone;
 it needs another to be known.

Leaves do oft give wind expression
 Yet neither ever claims possession.
Dust and dirt may give it shape
 as wind flows o'er nature's scape.

Slicing clean 'twixt tree and flower
 and rolling through the valley bower,
Bumping over rock and rill
 until it's calm and standing still.

The spirit, too, is like the wind,
 invisible yet destined
To be the breeze of inner mind
 with zephyred bliss to humankind.

Firewood

Wooded light stands darkly
    ready for expression.
Letting go the warmth within,
    giving up possession.

How powerful is this teacher,
    this lecture of the wood,
Remembering the gift of sod
    and light from a tree that stood.

It only takes a spark
    to change the wood to fire,
And feel the sun again
    in a golden lighted pyre.

Whoever holds a match or thought,
    not knowing how it ends,
Gets sulphured cries of pain;
    therein truth transcends.

In life and wood see the light,
    the heat and the fire,
Then live in the moment,
    as love becomes your choir.

Someone Said

Someone said, "Forgive him!" and tears
    welled in my eyes.
How do you forgive your son
    who's choosing now to die?

Someone said, "It must be hard," to see
    him struggle so,
Knowing that his life is short and you
    must let him go.

Someone said, "You'll understand," when
    you pray to God.
They're trying to be helpful, but I can feel
    the sod.

Someone said, "How is he?" Can I send
    him something now?
Cards and calls and letters become
    his passage prow.

Someone said, "Just love him," and things
    became all right.
I forgive my son,
    and bless his journey to the light.

Window Rain

Racing, chasing down the pane,
　　drops that started out as rain,
Some are fast and others slow,
　　nervous sliding to below.

Stopping, starting, this way that,
　　changing by another's splat,
Lenses into nature's gray
　　help define the type of day.

Streaking, leaking, lines of wet,
　　never staying, never set,
Trace their path before it's dry
　　to see a water butterfly.

No singing song of "go away,"
　　I truly want the rain to stay.
I miss it when it is not here,
　　to make my glass a chandelier.

Five Bells

Five bells for fair winds echo across the sea,
    salty mist anoints a passage by the key,
When spirit ship of time sails the trade winds free,
    the yards of arm and mast stretch far a lee.

Five bells for fair winds will always let you be
    aloft on the ropes until it's NOW you see.
No flotsam when a wake, no jetsam debris,
    the present is the current, not an eddy.

Five bells for fair winds, an Albatross decree:
    It's truth I'm soaring after. If you agree,
Ride the cresting wave, to see the I as we.
    Five bells for fair winds, a ringing destiny.

Ginger

She lives now in a wheelchair,
 aged by grace and not despair.
She once was light in song and dance,
 though now her steps are dream nuance.
She knows she is different now,
 yet mind remembers every bow,
With wishes and abandoned hope
 tucked within mind envelope
That once held honors for the pair
 when she danced with Fred Astaire.
We all go through this change of time,
 with added years above our prime.

I cannot leave you in this tale
 for you to think her spirit frail.
Ginger's heart is young and agile
 though her body seems now fragile.
Her inner light is in control,
 patient waiting for bell to toll
The numbered days for time's release
 when all the pain will finally cease.
It was a pleasure once again
 to honor her long-lasting reign
As queen of dance and radiance.
 I'll always be her audience.

Dry Brook

The rocks lie dry and lonely
   when the water does not run,
Recalling times of only
   wet, and sparkles in the sun.

New leaves and seeds lie waiting
   in a bed where water flowed,
Waiting rain's enervating
   spirit, life and growth bestowed.

When the rain drops from the cloud
   and trickles turn to stream,
Arid silence turns aloud
   again, to sing nature's theme.

Haven Green

There is a place in desert clime
    that resonates with earth's deep rhyme.
Where stringing greens of lace are hung
    to keep us cool from burning sun.

Old wrinkled pines root deep in ground
    and shed their needles all around
To quilt the surface of the land
    that we find comfort on the sand.

The needle grove is emerald soft
    with verdant hues from up aloft
Reflecting tones of tan and light
    embracing us in shaded bright.

And when the desert breeze glides in
    it gives a sound to where we've been
Within the page of nature's tome
    listening to a natural poem.

Hummingbird

A humming bird rests alone
    on a lilting leafless perch,
Surveying all the flowers in her
    sweetened nectar search,
But never looking back upon
    the path she just had flown.

Her satin cloak of colors glow,
    in iridescent hues:
Purple reds and yellow greens,
    and neon shimmering blues,
A radiance of under down
    shining from below.

O tiny bird with humming wing
    and resplendent aura bright,
Thy harmony of purring tones
    brings sound to celestine light.
You are an angel spirit bird,
    you hover, hold and sing.

Awareness

The darkness in the room
    spilled out through the door,
To meet the sound of surf
    smashing at the shore.

In the late of the night
    or the early of the morn,
I listened to the OM
    and heard the light be born.

Do all ask the question, Why?
    when lying near the sea?
Is the answer special
    that only comes to me?

The truth to the why
    comes deeply from within,
As I feel my tidal pulse
    and its crimson surge — the Din.

Be forever mindful of the now, as your
    spirit seeks the All.
Hold its rhythm in your heart and hear the
    Universe call.

Arrows From Heaven

The heart drum throb of ancient tribes
    transcends in timbre's pulse sublime
As cadenced rhythmic beat proscribes
    a nature past, but still divine.

Shoshone, Ute and Navaho,
    proud native hearts of desert west,
Hopi, Zuñi, Arapaho
    beat sacred drums for vision quest.

From heaven, then, come arrows gold
    to find their set within the heart,
So story old can then be told
    by feathers' stride 'long sacred dart.

The cricket calls in night's dark damp
    to lover and to lunar light
That shows the way to dreamers' camp
    and wings our minds for freeing flight.

Arcadian shafts, fluted points,
    painted ponies and shaman's chant
Reprise the Past and then anoint
    the drumming with a step courante.

When beat of heart and those of drums
    transform the time of honor due,
Ancestral rest then finally comes
    and spirit heart is birthed anew.

Anguish

Brahms in the sterile hotel room.
My naked body listens
and hears only the echo of infection
        in the city far below,
Its Circe call contaminating once again the
        ego wounds of want.

The space between the street
        and the music is vast.
So too is the chasm between wants —
        immense in its closeness,
        Divine in its distance,
And I've known it from the beginning.

Jack Frost

We much malign a draft of cold
        slippin' round a window old,
A chilling dash of winter clime
        that paints a pane in ice of rime.

Without the draft and warmth within,
        the crystal etch could not begin.
So let us praise the weathered sash
        that lets us see a frost panache.

Martin Luther King

I had a dream the other night
and Martin Luther King was there.
He spoke in tones befit the wise
and asked me if I'd share
The news of how his dream came out,
since he had been away.

I told him times had changed somewhat
but the dream was still a dream
And somewhere in these many years was
progress, or so it seemed.
Tell me, he said, what has happened,
since he had been away.

We've legislated out the hate, I said,
but laws can't touch the mind,
If bias reeks within the heart,
there cannot be a human – kind.
It's still not true, he said,
for he had been away.

And then he said, where he is now,
there is no ONE color bright,
Not black or white, yellow or brown.
There is only a loving light.
It's the truth I lived, and live,
he said, as he went away.

Leaves

I now know why we call them leaves,
    too soon they fall when frosted thieves
Lure their green to red and gold
    in colors soft and dazzling bold.

Leafs drop from age and sometimes breeze
    to land beside the shrubs and trees,
Drifting, pillowed to the ground
    in crinkling, crackling, scrunching sound.

O leaves of branch and bush, behold!
    Your service lasts despite the cold,
Quilting warmth for creatures low,
    beneath the ground, before the snow.

Some leaves sail to lawns serene
    where children's smiles can be seen
Waiting for the rake and pile
    to leap upon and lie awhile.

But soon the crumpled stems and flake
    are coaxed in rows for match to make
A downy flame and spired smoke,
    incense of honor to the oak.

Then barren trees stand naked, strong,
    to slice the wind of winter's song,
Leaning forth from bending blow,
    then snapping, weaving to and fro.

I know there is a message here,
     where trees with leaves at end of year
Soon molt their husk of leafy sheen
     for other seasons to be seen.

Trees and man are oft alike:
     In time each sheds their aging haik;
What's left in silhouette pristine
     is life anew in spirit green.

Night Walk

You know the warmth a chill can bring,
 when night walk sees the moon and ring,
As thistle-flowered clouds drift by
 the orb of gold, a quarter shy.

It is the sun's low angled light
 that comes from space, tho out of sight.
Beneath, above, below the Earth,
 somehow we move around its girth.

Night walks will oft give pause to see
 the peeking stars forever free,
Twinkling terse, through atmosphere
 as pin of light and poet's tear.

I stopped to watch the silvered loop
 as circles moved in golden hoop
Around the lunar cyclic globe
 to give the sky an aura robe.

But like the night, I must move on,
 returning to the comfort yon.
Embracing rings of lunar shine
 inspires walks in night's dark time.

She Is Resting Now

She is resting now, for only her body died.
　　Remember long her smile and duty done
　　with pride.
Honor now her choice and call it — a destiny.
She joins a noble roster of those who died
　　at sea.

She is resting now, in a light of another place
　　in Elysian Fields of Navy blue and waves
　　of gentle grace.
There are many there in uniform, who lived
　　once before
And crossed the veiled threshold, in peace and
　　in war.

She is resting now, find comfort in the fact
　　that service to her country was a willing
　　final act.
Keep faith with her and others and never ever
　　yield,
Be reminded by the poppies and a place called
　　Flanders Field.

She is resting now, a warrior's sleep is won
　　with echoes of a bugle call and taps at
　　Arlington.
Find a way through the tear, and breathe
　　another sigh,
And mark her life with honor, as we salute
　　good-bye.

*In honor of Navy Lieutenant Kara Hultgreen who died when her
F-14 jet crashed during carrier practice off the California coast.*

Old Woman

I watched her cry, old woman she,
        standing, where she should not be,
In the rubble of what was home
        memories crushed beneath the stone.

O justify, ye born of womb,
        the carnage and the massive tomb
That war does bring to distant land,
        tho nearer than some understand!

See first her tears that have no streak
        then watch and hear her silent shriek
That tells of bombs and guns and pain
        and soiled hopes with red bloodstain.

An aging face with wailed cries
        wrinkled pallor of failed tries
To be a mother keeping peace
        when the killing will not cease.

Do not fear this harmless image
        it's another civil scrimmage.
Forget its pain and division!
        Channel change the television!

Monterey Coast

The sand dune sky with
     drifts of blue.
Stately pines
     monuments — new.

The above is below
     the within without,
As breasted coast
     twists about.

One side is land
     the other sea
Crashing surf and
     spreading tree.

Stand at wonder
     of beauty raw
Monterey coast
     enthusing awe.

Oaken Nest

Who picnics here 'neath Druid Oak
and sees the rhyme of nature pass
Between the folds of spirit's cloak
among the leaves, within the grass?

I stop to lean on walking staff
and wonder 'bout this place serene.
Its magic is its epitaph.
I pray my gaze won't intervene.

A bench or two for those to dine
on sweetened breeze and lovers' kiss.
When sealed pure with amber wine
it lingers in a lasting bliss.

There's music in this oaken nest
for those aware of fairy glen.
A caution when you take your rest:
It opens up your dreams again.

Dale Turbush

Print 36/75

The painting framed upon the wall
   had rising mist and waterfall,
To draw my spirit to its plane
   and let me play in its domain.

Celestial peaks of snow and Stream
   majestic crests, drawn from a dream
Lit by a glow that's from within
   a place the artist must have been.

Surreal in its radiant truth
   reminding me of place of youth
When time did not infringe the heart
   and gave each moment a new start.

Hold fast, a vast old ecstasy
   that lingers in a mystery.
The painting has the sound of "OM"
   and a light that calls you home.

A Healing

A side a hallowed pew of stone
sprout Bluets' blooms in close embrace
Remembering a healing time
    with flowers blue in clustered lace.

Before this time and this wonder,
    this granite seat engendered thought
Of nature, 'long with tranquil tones
    from rippling rill where dreams are
    caught.

Then family! friends! One! One the same,
    stood loving strong, invoking light
From far off places, deep within,
    where miracles and cures unite.

From healing hands with gratitude
    drop sacred grains of martyred ground,
And there upon next warming spring
    the tiny Bluets could be found.

Come see with me the Bluets' bells
    and know the tiny bluish bloom
As delicate and messenger
    of healing hope from nature's womb.

Valentine

I remember when
    in another time
Two hearts in tune
    and in our prime
Embraced this day
    with card and rhyme.

But this is now
    a memory, though
As wishes fade,
    yet still I know
The feelings of
    sweetheart and beau.

Serendipity

Two strangers sat and talked
    of purpose first — then profession.
Obsession.
Concession!
Listening!
Learning!
Discussion wrapped in hope.
    A mental trunk
    of need and mind
    to move beyond regression.
Two strangers left as friend —
    a wonder how the mind can bend.

Loss

O memory! Do not grab the heart.
Hide the ache within; do not impart
A holding link. Loose the tightened rein
   the way you do when loss causes pain.
Give hurt its head and let it run free
   within the heart, tho mind may decree,
"It is mine, this grief! Leave it alone
   for me to hold and gnaw to the bone,
Beyond the cord of agitation."
   Ne'er let it be a consecration
Of what expectant hope desires.
   Let it be what it always sires,
A light of present love, forever
   bright in the thought of ending never.
Loosing from the mind a pulsing throb
   that holds unto self a tearful sob.
O memory! Loose thyself in love,
   recreate the joy, when glow above
Frees, upon a time the oversoul
   It knows a love in time must extol
Freedom to be, and in the living
   come gifts to see the joy in giving.

Rosebush

I saw a rose before its bloom
    within a bush of thorn,
Invisible, yet crimson bright,
    hopeful to adorn
A table vase or lover's heart
    with grace upon a morn.

Until red bud unfurls forth
    in aromatic rose,
Few will see the flower there
    ready to compose
A blossomed stem of prickling points
    and barbs sharp juxtapose.

But as the warmth of spring resumes
    and the cosmic colors flow,
The scarlet of the silent stalk
    begins its sanguine grow
And dabs the bush in beauty
    with red roses in tableau.

Snow Flower

A many-petaled flower of white
    nesting in the crystal light
Of ice and snow upon the green,
    a feast of beauty never seen.

Embrace the white of blossom cold.
    It softly lays in frosty bold
Within the freeze that decorates,
    yet gives a warmth that radiates.

A special flower in the snow?
    Or something else we do not know.
It matters not, for what is there
    is evergreen as torchère.

Candle

A candle wick charred black
    evidence of a flame.
When its light returns will it be the same?

Fire hides within
    a waning string of ebony.
Or is it somewhere else,
    a melting, waxing mystery?

Cry of the Blue Whale

They breach and play in lumbered grace,
    these ocean mammals of the pod.
We seek to slay in hunting chase,
    we human mammals of the sod.

O hear the strings of sighing heart,
    a woeful cry of noble Blue,
The whale's song, lament at start
    that tells of tears and numbers few.

Shafts of steel with harpoon tip
    free azure spirit from the heart.
A sharpened stab and flesh to rip,
    a carcass blue to take apart.

Now go beyond the screech of fear,
    and hear their talk in tender tone
That whales speak when traveling near
    seafaring families unbeknown.

Leviathan, great blue whale,
    sing your music for us to hear
The symphony of ocean tale,
    with violins in hydrosphere.

Someday your song will oft be sung
    by kindred kinds of land and sea
And maybe then you'll teach your young:
    Fear not mankind, he'll let you be.

The Poet Eye

I choose to honor a belief —
　　a tender touch of power
And ne'er decry a modern Muse
　　that builds a poet's tower.

Fill its loft with textured words
　　and litanies of emotion,
Can it be the sentient spire of
　　Calliope's magic potion?

A daughter then of ancient Zeus,
　　with songs of amethyst,
A Bacchus guild, now precious gem,
　　once facets of a myth.

Likes attract, as lovers know,
　　tho awkward at the start,
Easier said than ever done,
　　this sharing of a heart.

But there are secrets to be kept,
　　under rhyme and sub the rose.
Fables of a poet birthing,
　　loving, seeking to compose.

A poet's task is clearly known:
　　Bring image to expression,
Write it down, then take it back,
　　seek wisdom in impression.

'Tis strange for me this wedded gift
 that newly seeks its time
Through the tumble of a phrase
 and rhythmic lighted rhyme.

Write I will, because I trust
 the singing of a bell
With scarlet tones of ringing truths
 that others cannot tell.

Two Deaths

There is a place of cuddling comfort
    and dancing Peaceful wonder,
Where bumps and bruises cannot hurt
    and toys and crayons never break,
Where pillow fights and giggles last,
    and frosting's taller than the cake.

Where teddy bears talk in colors
    and puppies wait to play.
Where candy is for breakfast
    and presents fill the room.
Where no one knows what fear is,
    no shadows can consume.

This special place is one of peace,
    of grace, and joy and games,
Where all the mothers of the past
    hold children who die young
And make for them a breasted warmth
    and memories always fun.

I believe that in this lighted place,
    there's no need to understand
How another takes a life
    and causes innocence to die,
But it does make me more aware
    of the child in all who cry.

Then truly does my judgment fade,
    and anger change to light.
When love is unconditional,
    forgiving then is pure.
Even so, my heart is heavy
    and I cry and cry some more.

The Witness

Be the witness, the one to see
that recognition sets all free
To be the grace expressed as art,
tho caution's mind was there at start.

Be the witness, indulgent friend
to help the dream of one transcend
Beyond the cord of nourishment
before the ego's banishment.

Be the witness to the present
gossamer gowned with love intent.
See the gift, unconditional,
inspired thoughts subliminal.

Be the witness, a grounded force
to help the spirit stay the course.
It's the truth, a clarion call,
if one succeeds, then so do all.

Waxpaper Morning

I love a waxpaper morning
 when nothing seen is clear.
Misty clouds descending,
 shrouding without fear.

What was, in light, crystal sharp
 dissolves in weaving gray.
When wafting, floating fog comes in,
 silhouettes can play.

The flowers thanked the mist
 for the shower of the cloud
And said this hazy dew
 would make their blossoms proud.

Then spearing through the wetted dim
 came warming rays of sun
And coaxed the mist to leave the ground,
 and now the day's begun.

Wind Song

I woke to hear the wind in words
    when the garden chimes would sing,
A gentle song of hanging bells,
    the music pealing in its ring.

Resonating other chimes,
    let the roaming wind sing too
And share a chorus of its soul,
    as rushing currents blew anew.

Modern mind with all its science
    dares not see wind as spirit.
Its view is one of isobars
    so the conscious mind won't fear it.

Native peoples of Gaia's breast
    know wind as spirit brother,
Sister too, from all directions,
    sourcing from the Father-Mother.

Listen silent to the sound
    as the wind moves through the trees.
The leaves and boughs become the reeds
    when zephyrs play the wooden keys.

Each flowing song of roving wind
    is the cosmos coming forth,
Gusting, soothing, steady, cooling
    from East and West, and South and North.

Then comes the time when all is calm,
    and currents stop to hear
The sound of love from nature's heart,
    renewing blowing balladeer.

Winter Morning

Mountain village in winter's grasp
delighting all who choose to know
What pleasure comes from steady cold
and sifted, powdered, fallen snow.

Drifted, diamond dunes of white
cover roof and tree and trail
With crystal sparks from nature's heart,
a blanket ode to season frail.

The rising sun and light announce
a crisp beginning to the day,
But soon the shine will melt the frost
of tiny stars in ice plié.

Long shadows cast by breaking dawn
create some grays upon the bright
From stands of aspen tall and straight
peeking, poking through the white.

Cold, early, hurried people trudge,
with crunchy steps on shoveled way,
Their rhythmic puffs of huffing breath
vanish with the warmth of day.

Too soon day ends with dusk, then night.
New cold invades the valley low
And far above, majestic peaks
crown the village 'neath winter's snow.

Yosemite

Does thou know how this place began when
time was young and visions cast?
Great glaciers met with granite dreams
of pinnacles and vistas vast.
They sculpted stone with noble peaks
and smoothed the valley floor.
They added cold a crystal stream
and falls to fill it evermore.
With every step and every turn
the breath is held by nature's grace
To reach within to All That Is
and consecrate this holy place.
Release your soul to soar above
and glide the drifting course,
Caressing all dihedral walls,
searching for a celestial source.

Does thou not know whose hand it is
that cradles in majestic awe
The spirit's quest for loving light
and binds all beauty evermore?
Thundered mist in sunlight prism,
rainbows bending beyond the mind
To rest its gold within our hearts
when rapture touches humankind.
Yosemite is not from here.
It's borrowed from another realm
Reminding eye of inner sight
in visions that will overwhelm.
Invoking nature's seed of rhyme
that nurtures life from out the stone
And finds the pathway to the source
is guided by the beauty shown.

Wishing Star

In dreams,
> in sleep,
>> my heart
>>> you keep.
>>>> To love,
>>> to feel,
>> to hold,
> to heal.

It's there,
> a star,
>> a light,
>>> afar.
>>>> A beam,
>>> a bliss,
>> a call,
> a kiss.

A wish, a wish, a wish.

A hope,
> a need,
>> a want,
>>> a plead.
>>>> A point
>>> of light
>> above
> in night.

A guide
    to be
        for you
           and me.
                O hear
           my heart
        when we're
    apart.
A wish, a wish, a wish.

Transcend
    this love,
        this star
           a dove.
                In space
           to shine
      as love
    of mine.
For you
    at night
        I am
           a light.
                A beam,
           a bliss.
      It's all
    a kiss.
A wish, a wish, a wish.

Dawn Song

Before the dawn, below the light
There is a time that still is night.
A morning dark festooned with song
in arias from avis throng.
A choral mirth and melody,
a whistling chanting rhapsody.

When rising orb bursts from the dim,
the song and light become a hymn
As flashing streaks of morning sun
ignite the shore and summit run.
Then bleaching light and harmony
absorb the darkness from the sea.

Soon colors shine from leaf and bloom,
their fragrant scents belie perfume.
When flowers reach to touch the glow,
the dew upon is lit flambeau.
Refracted rays of golden bright
bring out the rainbow from this sight.

Like the bloom, the mornin' flowers
into a day of lazy hours,
But nothing like the early morn
with its cantata to adorn
The heart of nature and her tone
that lets you know you're not alone.

Inner Storm

Some storms rage near and some far off,
    mine in where the heart is soft!
Between the beats, an ache portends,
    a tempest screams, no grief transcends
To higher realms, abated strife,
    and thickened tears to cut with knife.
I know not how to ease the pain
    nor all the fear we have constrained.
O agony of crafted cause,
    the soul is left in diapause.
It must be mine, this empty fear
    as feelings cloud with thoughts unclear.
Spirit light, take this fate from me,
    the darkness holds my agony.
I cannot be this death for long
    for I can hear a healing song.
It's on the other side of pain,
    and there's the joy that keeps me sane.

Tribal Lands

Some hardened stones are all that's left
    of tribal lands of long ago.
Yet knowing tongues now speak of times
    when native hearts again bestow —
A sacred cleansing at earth's breast
    with blue corn hallowed on the ground,
And thanks go out from modern minds
    acknowledging a pulse profound.

Distant brother, come share the blood
    of pale skin and ancient shame.
Trust long has bled, as casualty
    of broken treaties that proclaim –
The word of some was as the sand
    when empty wind would fly its course
And wipe the promise from the heart
    when soldiers took with no remorse.

Gentle sister of grassy plain,
    help calm the atavistic rage
That lingers as our history.
    Release its curse with smudging sage —
And see the smoke then dissipate
    the agony of saddened past
That hardened into crusted doubt
    when lands were taken that were vast.

The Legacy

We are the ancient ones of yore
    as we were you in times before
We seek to tell of futures past
    so you can know illusions cast.
This is an epoch time of change
    with energy that may seem strange,
That permeates the planet Earth;
    enlightenment will be its birth.
As Gaia nears millennia,
    and solar song rests at La,
The tone of Being harmony
    is octave sequenced to a Sea.
Once upon a scaled clef
    there is a void of space that's left
That takes you to another line
    then tunes your being out of time.
Freedom then may source the essence
    leading you to luminescence.
When mind accepts what is real,
    frightened soul begins to heal.
It is our joy to bring the ONE
    to human bodies just begun,
But then the task is up to you
    to track the heart and thus imbue
The character of humankind
    away from matter unrefined.
Choose to be unconditional,
    life is ever transitional,
Be forgiveness and forgiving,
    be receptive in receiving,
For in the letting go of stuff,
    the Universe presents enough.

Many "onces" upon a time,
    we saw thy plight of inner rhyme
And sent you light from space arcane
    so harmony you could sustain.

We oft will feel your soul within
    as pure creation without sin.
An arrow term of "off the mark,"
    your misconception since the Ark.
There is no sin when all are born,
    just angels' song to mark the morn
And sing thee to thy frequency
    so you may fill your destiny.
Remember back to long ago,
    before this time and this ego,
A spark of thought from primal source
    created you from dust resource.
Once upon descending spiral
    into matter from the astral,
You made a promise to return
    and share the love of your sojourn.
Do not be now disappointed,
    know thyself as one anointed.
Be the harbinger of healing,
    know there is no lonely feeling,
Accept the ones we self-create
    and then our children emulate.
They are the ones who seek a time
    when balance reigns and hearts will rhyme.
Release them to explore the new
    that they may BE their spirit true,
Beyond the skin of history
    deciphering their mystery.

Accept these changes like a child,
　　know the heart is undefiled,
When moving into loving light
　　there is no comfort like this might.
Cease the cycle of wanting more,
　　that binds your greed in hate and war
And blinds you to law of love
　　and stems your journey to above.
To those who grieve when epitaph
　　is said for souls who pass then laugh,
The body lone holds essence of
　　the spirit snug in fleshy glove,
But when release is finally here
　　there is no death to hold in fear,
Celestine mind is joyful clime
　　much different from your paradigm.
Here thought and you are seen as one
　　effulgent aura, gleaming sun.
There's paths and bends to flowered field
　　where reds and blues and eau de nil
Abound in vibrant rainbow light
　　to please the spirit and excite
The stars to twinkle from within
　　embraced by all the seraphim.
As you attain just one resolve,
　　choose lustrous love where all evolve
Into a beam of holy light
　　that bands the darkness from the night.
We, the ancients, invoke afar —
　　BE only love, that's what you are.